Artesitas

Maricela Griffith

To order additional copies of this book, contact:
Xlibris
844-714-8691
www.Xlibris.com
Orders@Xlibris.com

ISBN: Softcover   978-1-6641-4497-2
        EBook   978-1-6641-4496-5

Print information available on the last page

Rev. date: 06/21/2022

Artesitas

Written and Illustrated by:
Maricela Griffith

DEDICATION

To my precious jewels, my mother Maria de Jesus Varela Gomez
de Sanchez, and my brother Aldo Sanchez Varela.

Mother

Finally, you are free, free from the prison of your thoughts.

Free from oppressions and responsibilities.

If you believe that you comply with your sons and daughters, then you are free.

If you believe that you comply like a wife and mother, you are free.

You are free to live for you.

You are free to take a walk with your friends, your sisters, your brothers, your cousins.

Now you are to receive care and services. Now you have the time for your hobbies.

Now you have the time to be grandmother and be around your grandchild.

Now is the time for you, for your spirit, mind and body.

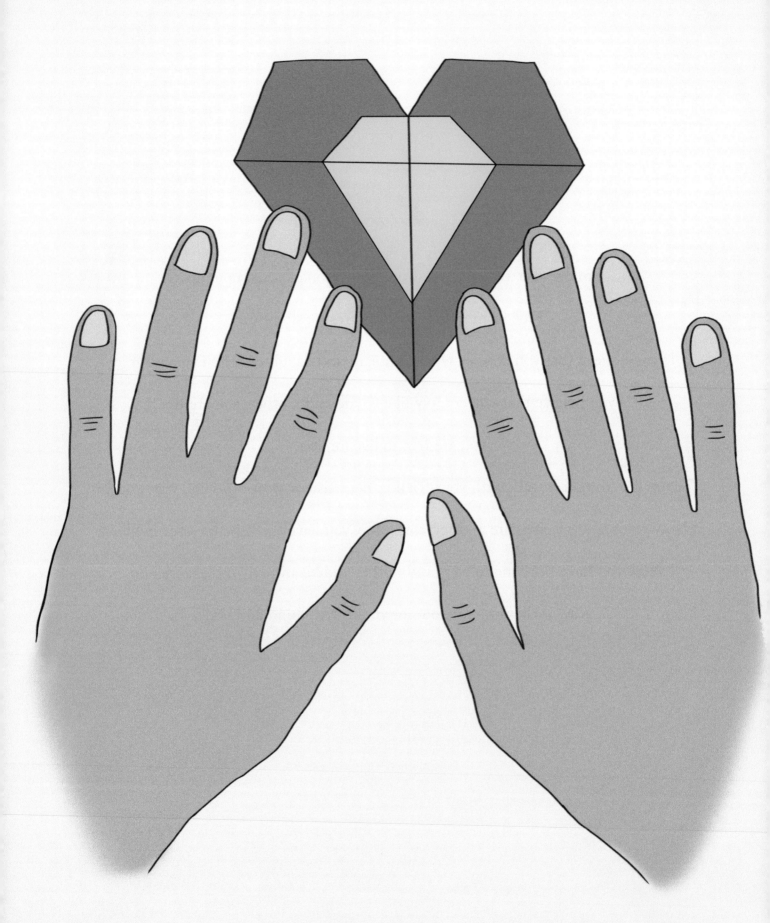

Dear Brothers and Sisters

We are united in blood forever.

I will have all of you present in my memory.

We will be together someday,

sharing as we are, a family.

We know each other very well,

before our partners.

We are a tied chain and we are bound for our parents.

Our lives are linked in our brotherhood.

Angel

I just want an Angel

The trust of its presence

An Angel to guide me

An Angel to advise me

So precious heart!

An Angel who smile me

An Angel who accompany me

A darling Angel who take care of my dreams

A primrose, Angel of pure love.

Clown

So adorable my Christmas child gift.

Little black hat and flower on it.

Some wrinkles in his eyes.

Red big nose, big red smiling mouth.

Plastic hands.

Different colors cloth body, with three cotton buttons in front of it

Plastic black shoes.

Dear Husband

I do not want to be your shadow, my Dear Husband.

I want to walk together happily in life.

I do not want you to go in front or behind me.

I want you to go with me by my side.

I want you to call me my partner.

I want us to celebrate our successes in harmony.

Both discover the sunrise.

Wait for the New Year together.

I want to know what is in your dreams.

I just want our love to be endless.

Think in me

When you feel alone, When you need companionship.

When your soul feel sad, When you feel frustration.

When nobody understand you, When nobody believe in you.

When you are sick, When people reject you.

When you can not left behind your vicious, When you feel stupid.

When you feel you are a traitor, When you feel you are dying.

When you are looking pardon, When you are lying in your sofa.

Think in me, I am here.

14

Yellow Rose

For a reason that I do not know you plant a yellow rose in the corner of our home in Kingston, Oklahoma, at the beginning in the division of the two paths.

We live there alone in the middle of the forest.

We live with Hickory trees, Oak trees, Pines, deer, turkeys and bobcats.

A land with ditches and ups and downs. We walked the Indian trail.

We rode in your old Jeep. We rode the horses. We worked with the cows.

We visited a Christian Church. We visited a little
church where we fit you and me only.

When we entered the little church a song sang for us.

We rode a water motor in Texoma Lake. One day we
saw with sadness our yellow rose death.

My heart was in pain and my voice exclaimed No! in anguish.

Something dies between us! Separation and death.

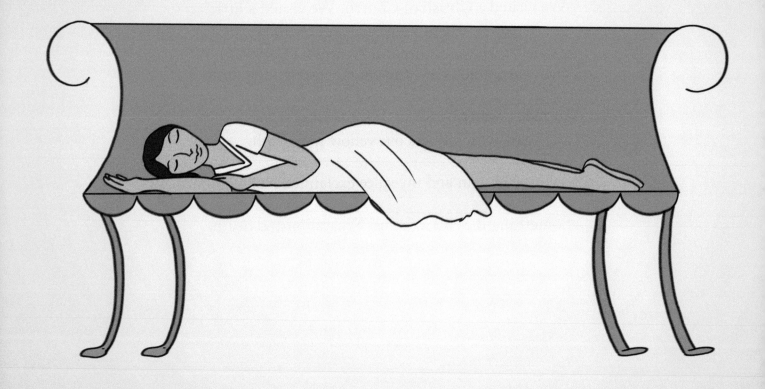

Friend

Lying in my couch, I did not have more comfort!

That thinking that I have a friend. I feel grateful.

This made all my happiness. This made all the difference.

Placidly I smile and sleep deeply to the next day.

Sweetheart

You are born in grace of God, by miraculous circumstances,

By a father and mother with little expectations, but they are rich in love and happiness.

You are our angel. You grew in spirit and heart too.

We have happiness with you. We found love with you.

We have fairness with you. You have such a precious heart.

We are blessed with you.

Daily

Movement and energy. Blow wind around.

White diamonds refresh the body.

Colors, perfumes and songs.

Discover new places. Comfortable sweet home.

Archangels, angels and cherubs at the table.

Love connections.

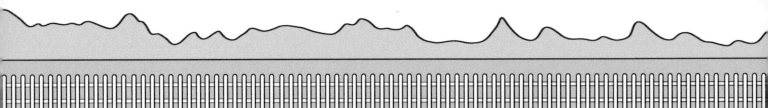

Weekends in The Peace Family Farm

I still see the corn or sorghum plantations, the lonely land and the tiny houses far away.

Our families drive from Reynosa city to the Peace family farm all weekends.

We never get bored or tired of being there.

We enjoyed playing too much to the "Hide and Found," "The Enchanters," "The Colors," running when it rained, and more children games with cousins, brothers and sisters.

My grandfather Bernabe Varela had a log cabin he made by himself.

The log cabin had a long bedroom and a kitchen with a chimney only.

He had 5 sons, 3 daughters and 42 grandchildren with my grandmother Maria de la Paz Gómez.

A big family that did not fit in the log cabin so we slept on the cars at night also.

In the afternoons, my grandfather cooked flour bread and my grandmother made lemon tea for us.

My grandmother told us tales and scary stories while we sat around her.

I like to see the stars in the sky and look for figures.

We listened to the coyotes, owls and other birds noises while listening to my grandmother. My grandfather sowed watermelon, melon, squash, tomatoes, peach, beans, corn, sorghum and more that he sold in the city and shared with us also.

We ride the wagon to other farms or the water dam to have picnics there and take a bath. When we came back, we hid ourselves if our clothes were red because of the bulls eating close to the paths. We had music and parties.

The Sunday's afternoons we returned to the city to continue our work and studies.

Life

Life is like a storm. Passes like water running off,

cleaning everything it encounters, after that nothing will be the same.

Like giant waves in the sea that cover everything,

it interrupts, whips, washes, purifies,

after that came the calm. If we last after the final, only memories will stand for us.

If we endure the trial, glory wreaths for those who pass the tests.

Awakening

Millions of diamonds reflect over the water when the sun kisses the earth.

Animals noises and hums alert the people and other animals.

Trees and plants open the leaves and petals.

For everybody is a new day to live.

A day in the sea

Only sand, blue sky, white clouds and sun.

The waves play without tiredness back and forth.

I can feel the heaviness of the water when I walk on it.

The water is passing my body to the sea,

Then coming back with force, foam, algae and salt.

Walking in the hot, humid sand, picking the shells.

Looking at the birds in the sky.

I barely can see the ships far away.

May and June weather

What a happiness at mornings and nights when it rains.

What freshness and what hot and humid when the sun came again.

The rainbow richness in color and brightness, appear
across side by side like a half crown.

Different tropical and desert trees, big fruits.

Leaves and flowers that cure and feed humans and animals. Distinct birds songs.

The heavy purple clouds suddenly appear in the sky,

Most of the time mornings, late afternoon and nights.

Those are the days in May rains and June storms in South Texas.

Leaving Fall to Winter

Running leaves over the street
Dancing leaves over the grass
Christmas almost here.

Running, dancing red, grape,
orange, yellow, brown leaves
over the trees.

Pecan, pear, and apple trees
November month is over here

Running, dancing, freezing,
leaves around above and down.

Dry, tall grasses and evergreen trees,
cows and horses around.

Running, dancing leaves over the rail.
Rusty, red, white, and green wagons.
Commerce and passengers wagons.

Freedom

Freedom to express myself. Freedom to be.

Freedom when the wind blows and I receive it. Freedom to walk on the earth.

Freedom when I am on the top of the mountain and I can see far around me.

Freedom in spirit. Freedom and peace together.

Faraway

I want to see faraway. To see what I can see more.

To look what I can look more. To find what I can find more.

I will see other people. I will discover new friends.

I will know other trees and plants. I will breathe different air.

Then I will feel new emotions. When I will perceive other oceans.

When I will experience new places. When I will observe new worlds.

Talking to myself

Passing through the life.

Why will I worry about who is ahead or behind me?

My thoughts are not others thoughts.

My ways are not others ways.

My creations are not others creations.

My feelings are not others feelings.

My life is not others life.

Probably we will cross paths in the streets or conversations, interchanging information,

and we will hold for a time and after that we will continue our lives.

Nobody can take my place because everybody is unique.

I cannot take anybody's place because I have my place in life.

People do what they need to do and me too.

My Feelings

I could almost die, can not stop crying for what a thing represents to me.

When other people pass away feeling nothing for the same thing.

I can even tremble, chilling for what a thing represents
to me, and others look at me laughing.

It is the reason, I respect others feelings,

because nobody feels the same or for nobody represents,

the same thing that for me represents.

The Mask

I am grateful when under circumstances I can see who you are,

because on other days you put your mask to cover you.

Those days you choose to show your face and I said,

Thank you to you! For taking your mask out.

You think, you are showing the worst of you.

I am thinking, "Thank you!" and I am smiling.

You neither know nor care my gratitude for you.

This way you are taking me less responsibilities and less problems.

The charge will be light for me.

I will better focus on my goals. I will enjoy my life more doing my objectives.

Thank you my ex-friends, my brothers and sisters, my neighbors,

my business partners, my associates, my members.

If you do not listen or ignoring me,

you just making my way out of obstacles to see better my goals.

The Cape

I will hide myself in my cape to cover me from outside as a shell.

Where I feel protection and comfort.

I feel so happy and joyful.

I understand, I comprehend, and I am aware of the world.

We all have a thesaurus in our interior, awaiting for us to be discovered.

A great journey!

We first need to be quiet and listen to ourselves.

Stop running for a moment, listening to our minds, our hearts and spirits then flourish.

Express, create whatever you feel.

Raise yours winds and let your imagination fly and spread your magic to the world.

When you need it, just step out.

November the Second

It was the darkest night I had ever seen, only illuminated
by a red, blue, yellow, cloudy and shiny moon.

The view was desolate and the wind was gelid. There was a rare silence,

Suddenly a black cat, its back, arched forming what appeared to be
a burr. It cried. Grinding doors opened at Wells' cafeteria.

A woman dressed in black slowly comes through the door.

She had a black veil covering her face. She walked closely to the workers and said:

My happiness is, nobody knows when I will come!

November the first is "All Saints Day!".

This is when Tony was born. He is an angel which the Skeleton likes.

November the second is the "Day of the Dead."

Earlier Skeleton leaves her tomb, dressed in black to make friends and invite them
for a ride. A ride of no return! Wells, an auto parts company, had a big party.

Then arrived the beautiful woman dressed in black, soon she
was our friend. Anna, Maggie, Maribel, Alma, Martha and
Maricela, had a pleasant conversation about health.

Then arrived Eduardo, very much a leading man. Tony wanted
to scare the woman but he saw her indifference,

and he moved away to the other side with Mr. Don, a respectful gentleman.

Eduardo was alone, he always had a good posture and was
confident too. His hair was shiny dark and upright.

He stood up and invited her to leave without admiring her body and face.

The woman with an enigmatic smile accepted.

Since Eduardo did not know it was the Skeleton who took him.

Very late! Now he is crying for his girlfriend Astrid, who stayed
disconsolate in this world. The Skeleton laughed loudly and said,

"Poor Anna, Maggie, Maribel, Alma, Martha and Maricela.

They do not know when I will come for them."

Voices around me

Voices around me that do not let me think.

Voices that do not let me be myself.

Voices that are not quiet and will not be quiet at all.

Minds that think and talk constantly.

Those will not stop nor sleep.

Noises, movements, laughs unstopping.

There is not a quiet place until I arrive at my home, where I lock the principal door.

Fantasy Color Hair

In the fantasy of your dreams,

the color of your hair seams,

gold, silver, brown, black, red, purple, blue, pink, orange.

Done as a hairstyle with adornments tied in a bow.

It looks artistic.

You walk in the streets wearing your hair color.

It has something different, and it is your fantasy color hair, oils and scents.

Printed in the United States
by Baker & Taylor Publisher Services